Place Value

Key Skills in Maths for ages 5 to 7

Paul Broadbent

For Key Stage 1 of the National Curriculum in England and Wales, and Northern Ireland, and towards Level B of Mathematics 5–14 in Scotland.

Heinemann

Heinemann Educational Publishers
Halley Court, Jordan Hill, Oxford OX2 8EJ
a division of Reed Educational and Professional Publishing Ltd

Heinemann is a registered trademark of Reed Educational and Professional Publishing Ltd

Oxford Florence Prague Madrid Athens
Melbourne Auckland Kuala Lumpur Singapore Tokyo
Ibadan Nairobi Kampala Johannesburg Gaborone
Portsmouth NH (USA) Chicago Mexico City Sao Paulo

First published 1998

01 00 99 98
10 9 8 7 6 5 4 3 2 1

ISBN 0 435 02379 9

Produced and typeset by Celia Floyd
Illustrated by Cathy Hughes
Cover design by John Kelly
Printed and bound in Great Britain by Thomson Litho, East Kilbride, Scotland

Contents

Counting patterns   Towards Level 2/Level B
1   Snake patterns   Counting patterns to 20
2   Trains   Counting patterns to 50
3   Number square (1)   Counting patterns to 100
4   Number square (2)   Counting patterns to 100

Place value: TU   Towards Level 2/Level B
5   Picture gallery   Place value: TU apparatus
6   Rockets   Place value: expanded notation TU
7   Birds' nests   Number words to 100
8   Spaceships   Making 2-digit numbers

Place value: HTU   Towards Level 3/Level B
9   Hot air balloons   Place value: HTU apparatus
10   Trains   Place value: expanded notation HTU
11   Using an abacus   HTU numbers on an abacus
12   Windmills   Making 3-digit numbers

Addition:
using place value   Towards Level 2/Level B
13   Tower blocks   TU + U without bridging the tens
14   Puzzle tree   TU + U bridging the tens
15   Threading tens   Adding 10
16   Adding machines   Adding 100

Subtraction:
using place value   Towards Level 2/Level B
17   Stacking boxes   TU − U without bridging the tens
18   Hopping back   TU − U bridging the tens
19   Shorts and T-shirts   Subtracting 10 and 20
20   Subtracting machines   Subtracting 100: function machines including inverses

Rounding   Towards Level 3/Level B
21   Kites   Rounding TU numbers to the nearest 10
22   Fruit and nuts   Rounding HTU numbers to the nearest 10
23   Fishing   Rounding numbers to the nearest 100
24   Rounding robots   Rounding to the nearest 10 and 100

Ordering numbers   Towards Level 3/Level B
25   Railway stations   Ordering TU numbers
26   Rally cars   Ordering HTU numbers
27   Postcards   Ordering numbers
28   Three digits   Ordering numbers

Introduction

The Key Skills series provides attractive and varied photocopiable sheets to extend and supplement core schemes and other resources. The up-to-date content fits National Curriculum requirements and Mathematics 5–14 in Scotland, and covers a range of work appropriate from Reception to Year 2. Its blend of traditional and more open activities will help children improve their maths skills while discovering that maths can be fun.

The books have been designed for the busy teacher: quick and easy access to mathematical content, and simply worded sheets requiring minimal teacher intervention. The photocopiable format allows flexibility to differentiate between the needs of individual children. Although there is progression between worksheets, not every child will need to complete each sheet, whereas some children may need further practical activities before attempting a sheet.

It is important to ensure children understand the task before they begin, by discussing each sheet with them. Just pencils and colouring media are needed. For particular sheets, some children may benefit from the support of extra practical apparatus, such as counting aids.

It is important for children to talk about their mathematical activities. Sometimes discussion may be more valuable while a child is working and sometimes after a sheet has been completed. Help the children identify when it would be appropriate for them to discuss their work with others – a friend, an older child, small group or class helper – and encourage them to share with parents their enthusiasm in what they are learning.

Name _____

Snake patterns

Write the missing numbers.

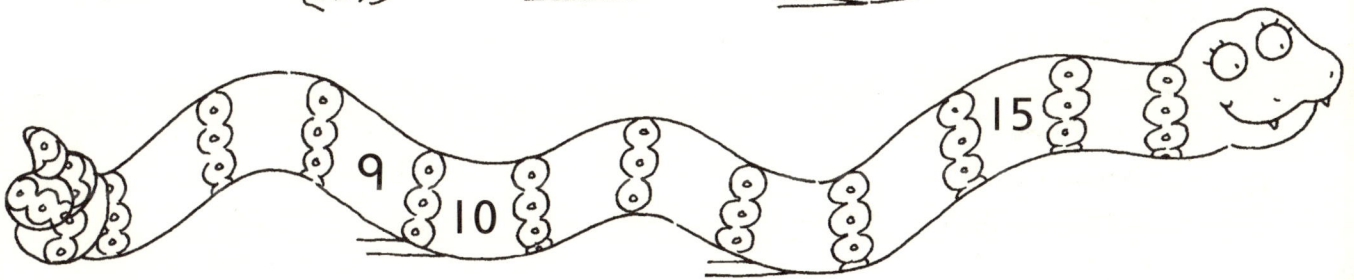

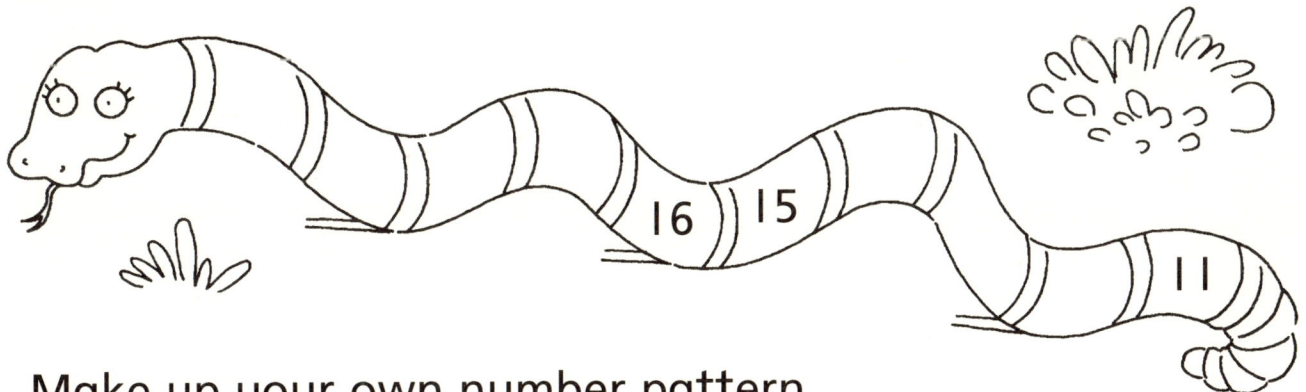

1 2 3 ... 8

17 16 ... 14 ... 8

9 10 ... 15

16 15 ... 11

Make up your own number pattern.

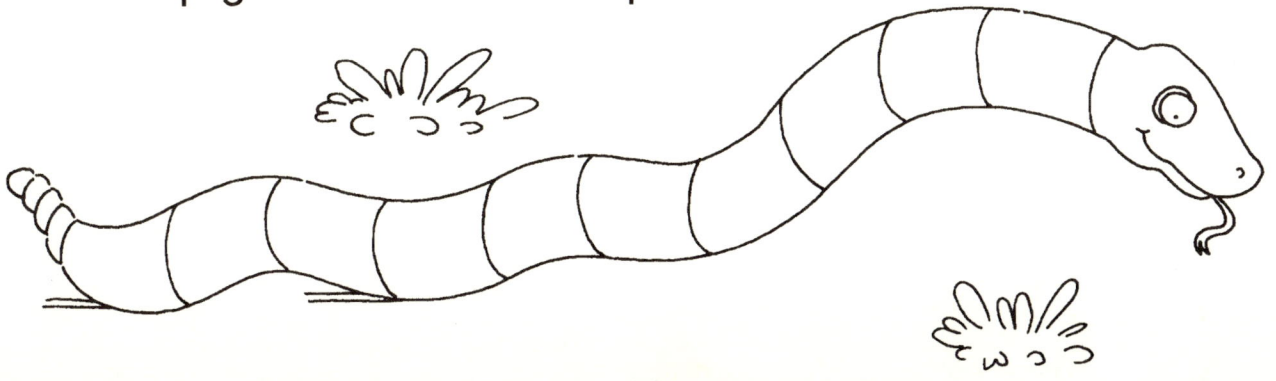

Counting patterns to 20

Name _____

Trains

Write the missing numbers.

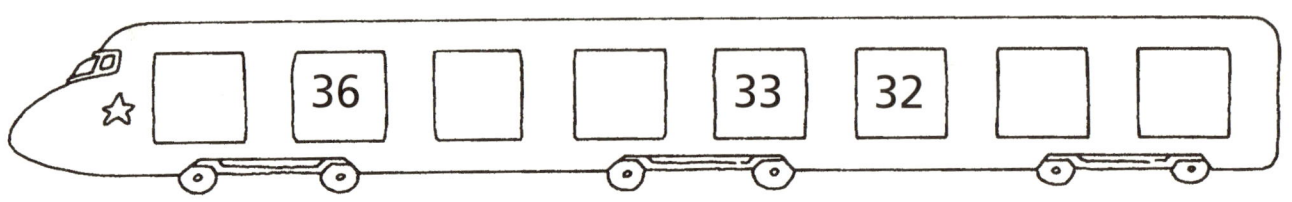

| 23 | 24 | | 26 | | | | 30 |

| | | 37 | 38 | 39 | | 41 | |

| | | 47 | 46 | | | | 42 |

| | 36 | | | 33 | 32 | | |

Make up you own number pattern.

| | | | | | | | |

Key Skills in Place Value at Key Stage 1
© Paul Broadbent 1998

Name _____

Number square (1)

Write the missing numbers.

1	2	3	4						10
11	12			15	16	17		19	
		23	24		26		28		30
	32	33		35		37		39	
	42					47		49	
51			54		56				60
		63	64		66		68		70
71	72							79	
		83		85					90
							98	99	

Colour the even numbers red.
Colour the odd numbers blue.

What do you notice?

Counting patterns to 100

Key Skills in Place Value at Key Stage 1
© Paul Broadbent 1998

4

Number square (2)

Write the missing numbers.

1	20	21	40		60			81	100
2	19		39	42		62			
3		23					78		
	17		37	44		64	77	84	
	25			56	65				
6	15						75		
		34	47	54			87		
		33		53	68				93
	12		49						
10	11	30		50		70	71		91

Colour the even numbers red.
Colour the odd numbers blue.

What do you notice?

Counting patterns to 100

Key Skills in Place Value at Key Stage 1
© Paul Broadbent 1998

Picture gallery

Write these numbers.

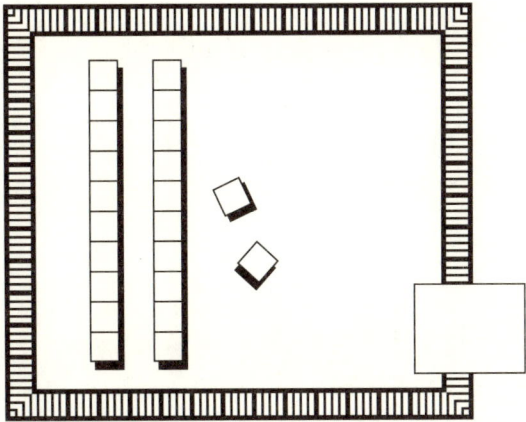

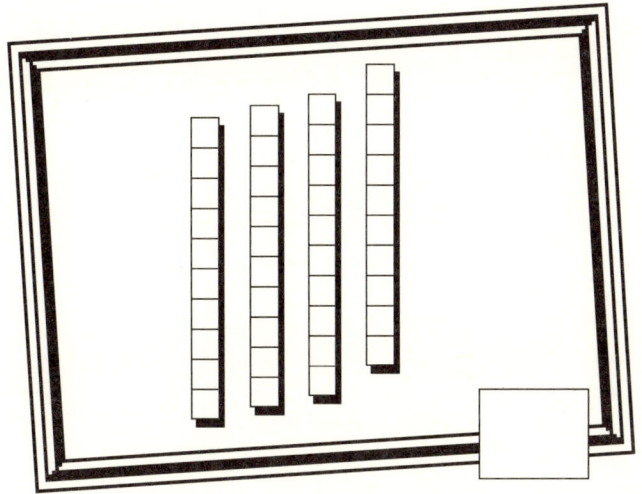

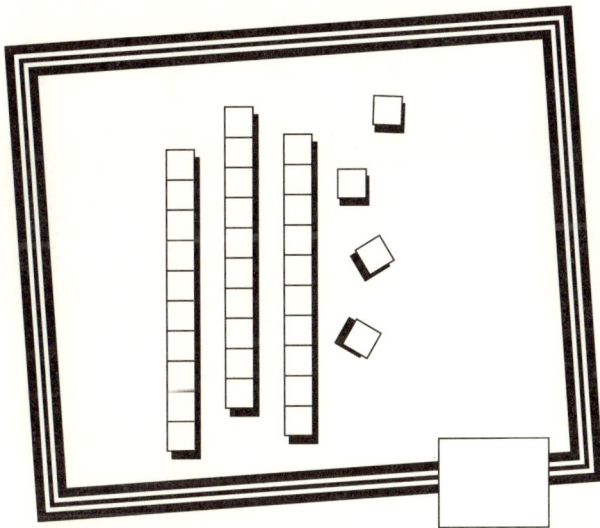

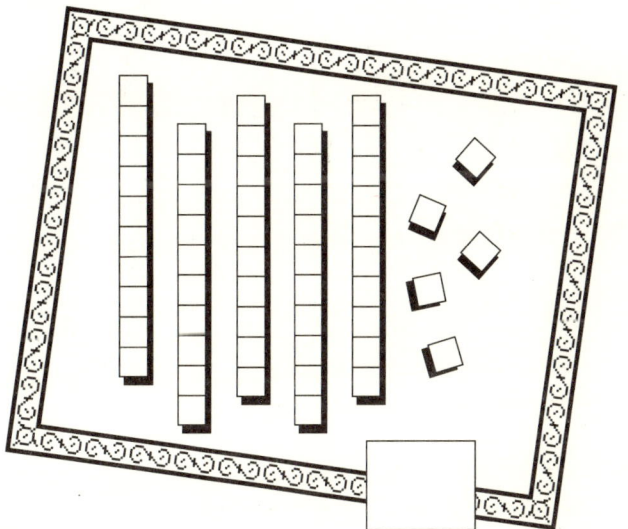

Draw pictures for these numbers.

27

36

Place value: TU apparatus

Rockets

Name _____

Write the tens and units.

3 7 = 3 0 + 7

5 2 = [ ] [ ] + [ ]

1 9 = [ ] [ ] + [ ]

3 4 = [ ] [ ] + [ ]

7 7 = [ ] [ ] + [ ]

9 6 = [ ] [ ] + [ ]

Write your own number.

[ ] [ ] = [ ] [ ] + [ ]

Place value: expanded notation TU

Key Skills in Place Value at Key Stage 1
© Paul Broadbent 1998

Name _____

Birds' nests

Match the birds to their nests.

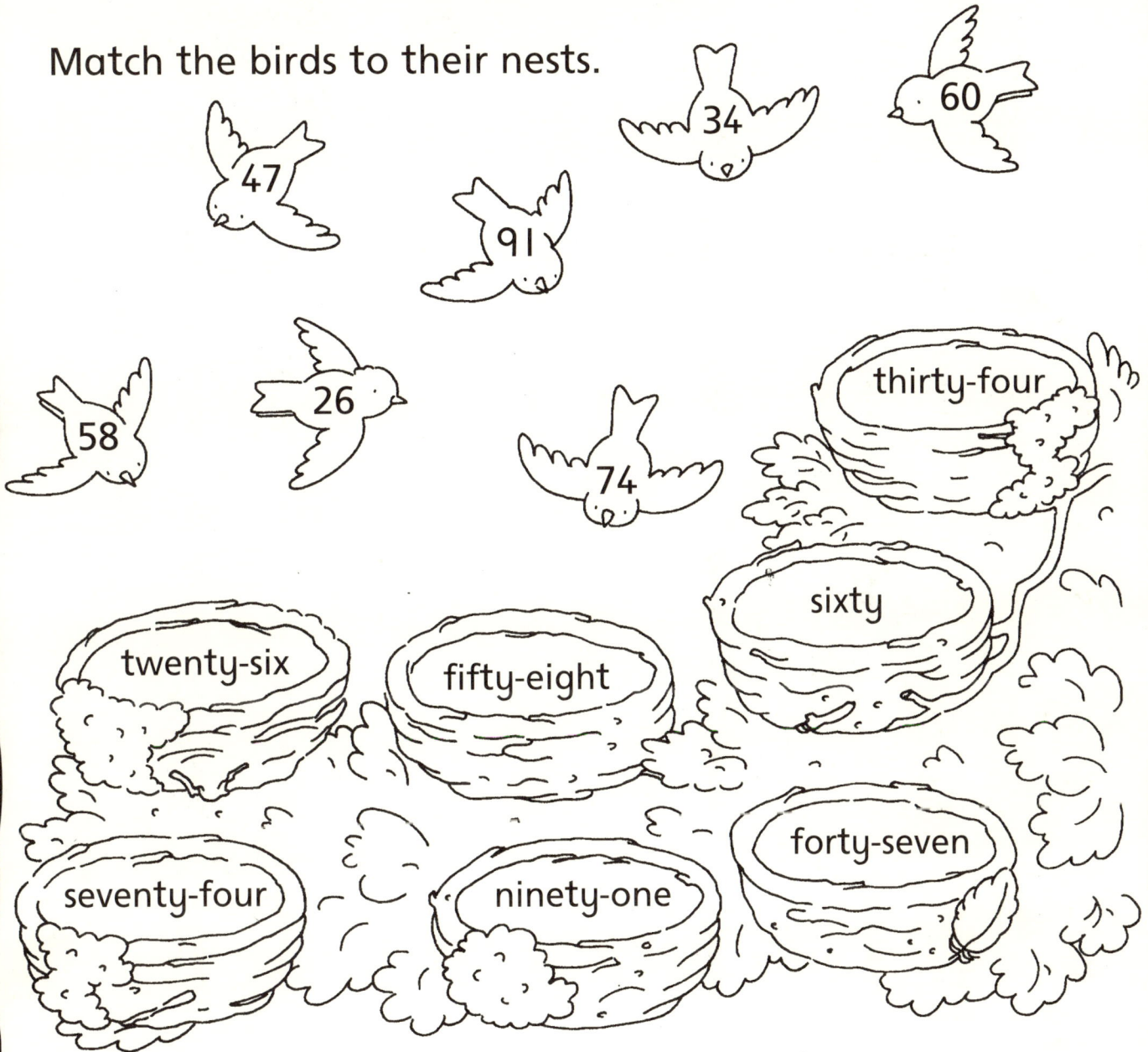

47   34   60

91

58   26   74

thirty-four

sixty

twenty-six   fifty-eight

seventy-four   ninety-one   forty-seven

Write these numbers in words.

36 _____   52 _____

64 _____   27 _____

49 _____   78 _____

Number words to 100

Key Skills in Place Value at Key Stage 1

Name _____

Spaceships

Make two-digit numbers.
Use the numbers in each spaceship.

Colour your largest number red.
Colour your smallest number blue.

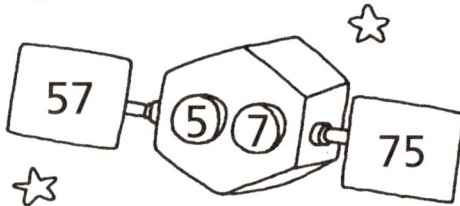

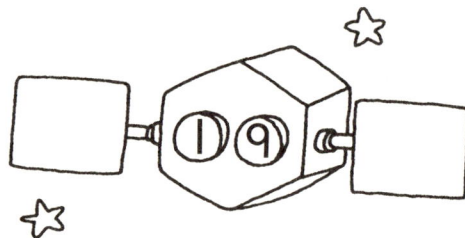

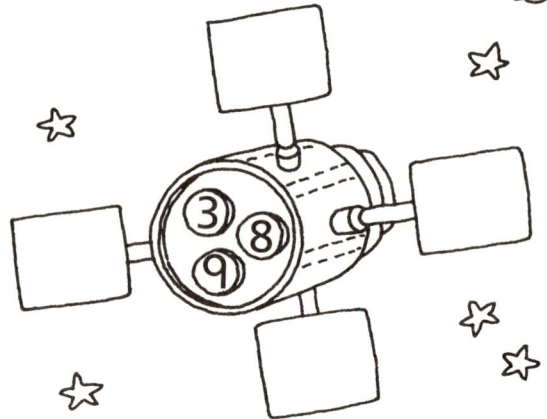

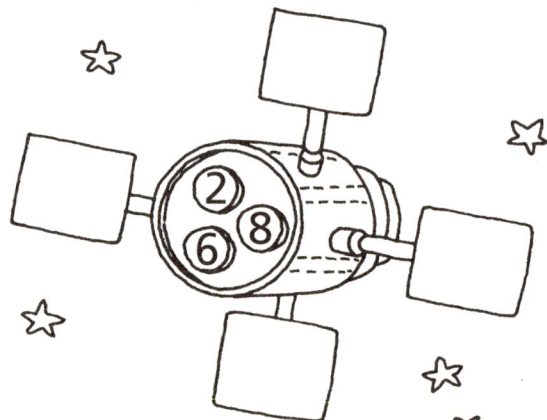

34

64   3 4   46
       6

36

57   5 7   75

4 6

5 2

1 9

8 3

3 8
9

4 9
2

1 7
5

2
6 8

Making 2-digit numbers

Name _____

Hot air balloons

Write these numbers.

Key Skills in Place Value at Key Stage 1
© Paul Broadbent 1998

Name _____

Trains

Write the hundreds, tens and units.

$342 = 300 + 40 + 2$

$629 = \boxed{} + \boxed{} + \boxed{}$

$431 = \boxed{} + \boxed{} + \boxed{}$

$758 = \boxed{} + \boxed{} + \boxed{}$

$974 = \boxed{} + \boxed{} + \boxed{}$

Write your own number.

$\boxed{} = \boxed{} + \boxed{} + \boxed{}$

Place value: expanded notation HTU

Key Skills in Place Value at Key Stage 1
© Paul Broadbent 1998

Name _____

Using an abacus

Write the numbers shown.

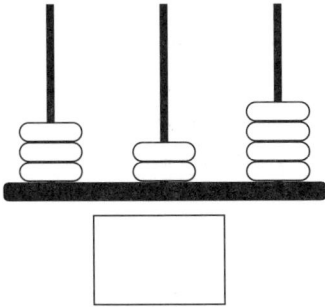

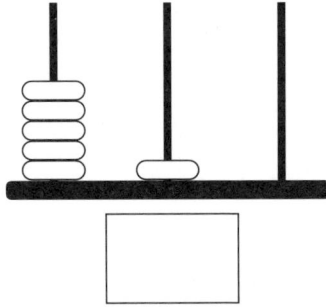

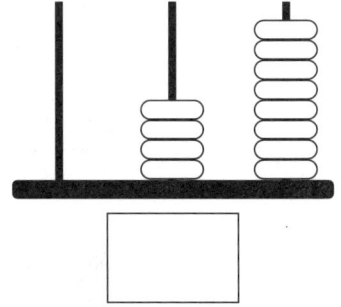

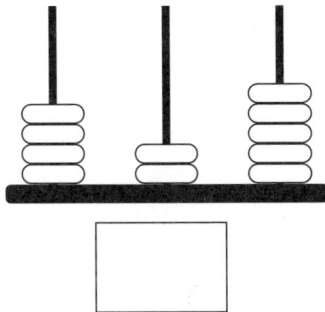

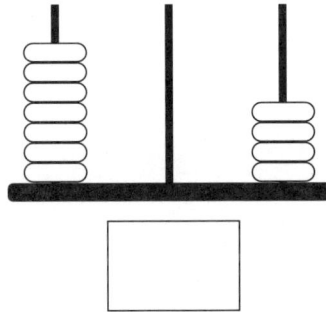

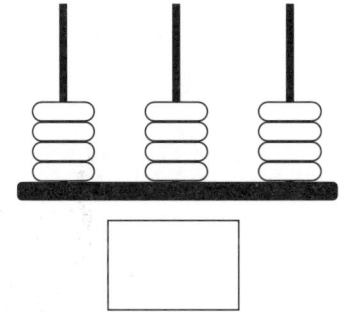

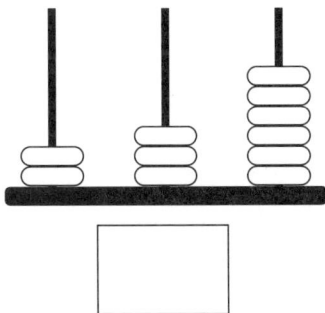

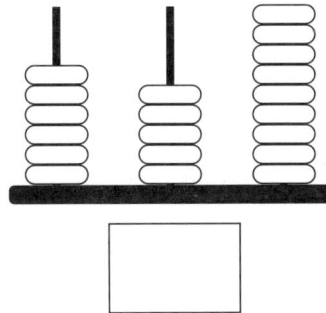

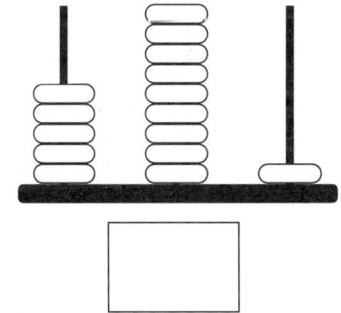

Draw beads to show the numbers.

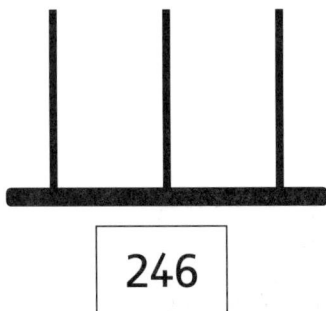

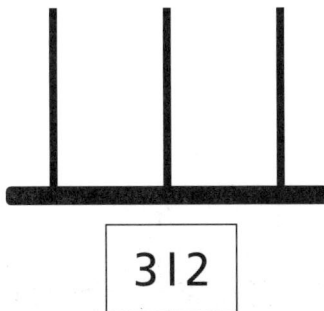

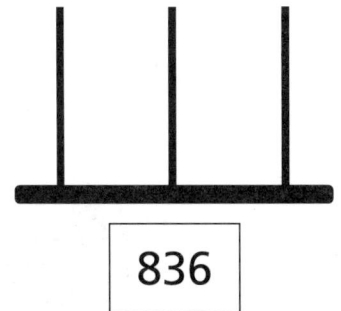

| 246 | 312 | 836 |

HTU numbers on an abacus

Key Skills in Place Value at Key Stage 1

Name _____

Windmills

Make three-digit numbers.
Use the digits in the sacks.

Write your largest number.

| 387 | 783 |
| 873 | 378 |

3 8 7

873

4 6 1

2 5 9

3 6 2

9 8 7

4 1 5

Making 3-digit numbers

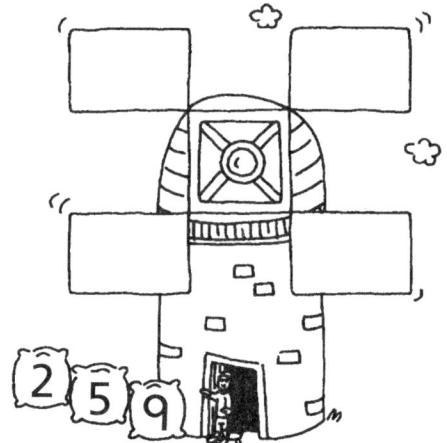

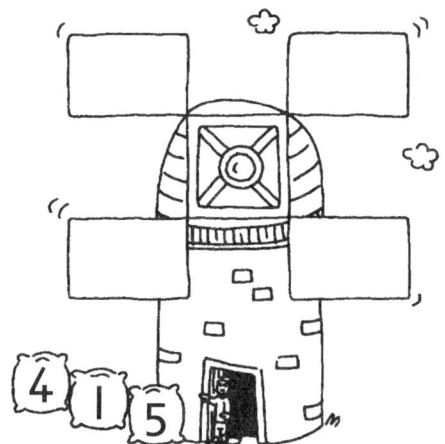

Name _____

Tower blocks

Write the answers.

6	+	3	=
16	+	3	=
26	+	3	=
36	+	3	=
46	+	3	=

4	+	3	=
14	+	3	=
24	+	3	=
34	+	3	=
44	+	3	=

5	+	2	=
15	+	2	=
25	+	2	=
35	+	2	=
45	+	2	=

2	+	4	=
12	+	4	=
22	+	4	=
32	+	4	=
42	+	4	=

4 + 5 =

44 + 5 =

7 + 2 =

67 + 2 =

2 + 6 =

82 + 6 =

TU + U without bridging the tens

Key Skills in Place Value at Key Stage 1
© Paul Broadbent 1998

Name _____

Puzzle tree

Write the answers in words.

36 + 8 | f | o | r | t | y | | f | o | u | r |

27 + 9

43 + 9

25 + 6

64 + 7

15 + 7

75 + 6

59 + 4

79 + 6

23 + 9

47 + 8

Write the number hidden in the tree trunk. ☐

Key Skills in Place Value at Key Stage 1
© Paul Broadbent 1998

Name _____

Threading tens

Write the missing numbers.

+10
→

15 → 25 → 35 → ◯ → ◯ → ◯

37 → ◯ → ◯ → ◯ → ◯ → ◯

52 → ◯ → ◯ → ◯ → ◯ → ◯

86 → ◯ → ◯ → ◯ → ◯ → ◯

105 → ◯ → ◯ → ◯ → ◯

Write your own starting number.

◯ → ◯ → ◯ → ◯ → ◯ → ◯

Adding 10

Adding machines

These machines add 100.
Write the missing numbers.

IN	OUT
37	137
52	
65	
40	

+ 100

IN	OUT
142	
207	
355	
190	

+ 100

IN	OUT
592	
770	
649	
408	

+ 100

IN	OUT
327	
543	
809	
677	

+ 100

Put in your own numbers.

+ 100

+ 100

Adding 100

Stacking boxes

Write the answers.

8 – 4 = ☐   7 – 5 = ☐

18 – 4 = ☐   17 – 5 = ☐

28 – 4 = ☐   27 – 5 = ☐

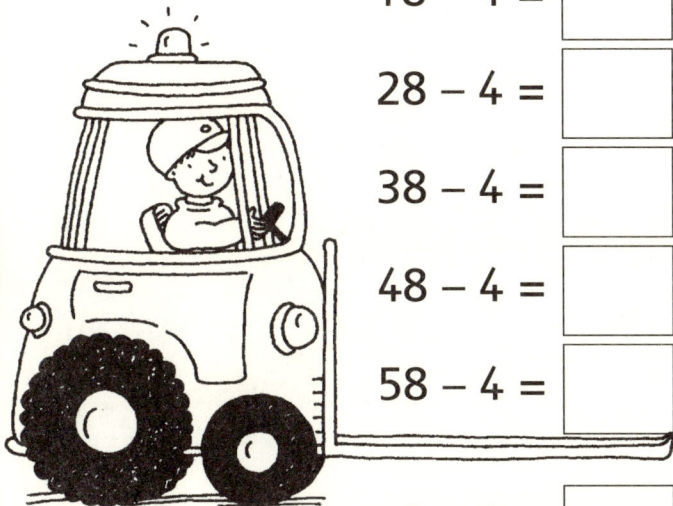

38 – 4 = ☐   37 – 5 = ☐

48 – 4 = ☐   47 – 5 = ☐

58 – 4 = ☐   57 – 5 = ☐

9 – 3 = ☐   6 – 3 = ☐

19 – 3 = ☐   16 – 3 = ☐

29 – 3 = ☐   26 – 3 = ☐

39 – 3 = ☐   36 – 3 = ☐

49 – 3 = ☐   46 – 3 = ☐

59 – 3 = ☐   56 – 3 = ☐

8 – 6 = ☐   7 – 2 = ☐   9 – 4 = ☐

88 – 6 = ☐   87 – 2 = ☐   89 – 4 = ☐

TU – U without bridging the tens

Key Skills in Place Value at Key Stage 1
© Paul Broadbent 1998

Name _____

Hopping back

This frog hops back to find the answer.

34 − 6 = [28]

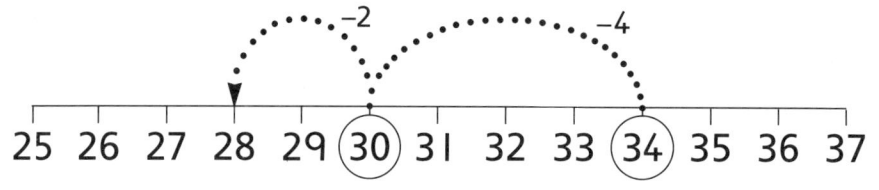

Use the number lines to help you.

43 − 7 = [ ]

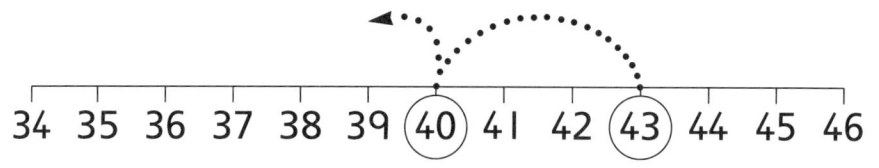

36 − 7 = [ ]

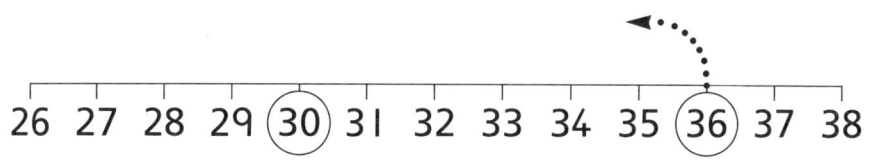

52 − 5 = [ ]

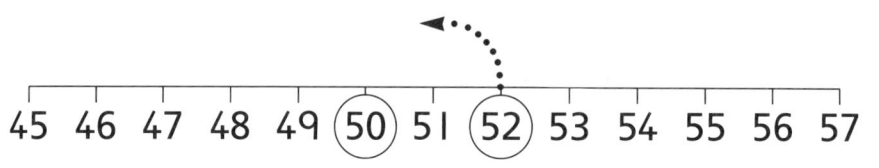

45 − 8 = [ ]

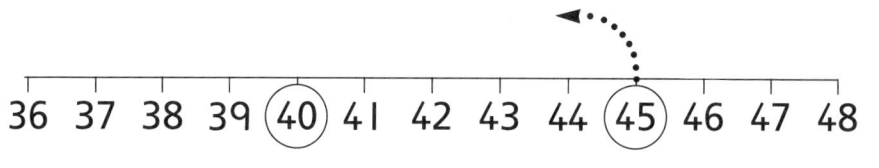

64 − 6 = [ ]

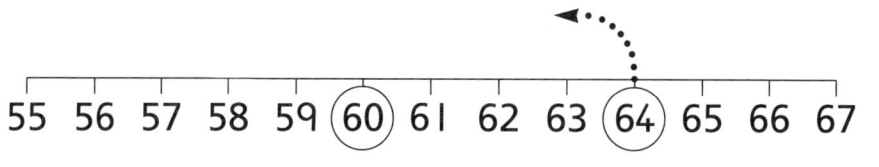

TU – U bridging the tens

Key Skills in Place Value at Key Stage 1
© Paul Broadbent 1998

Name _____

Shorts and T-shirts

Work out the sums.
Colour the shorts and T-shirts to match.

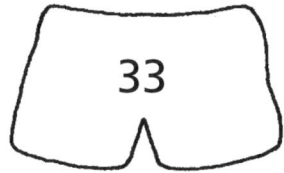

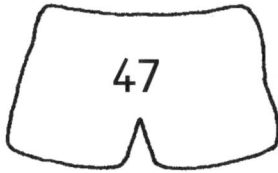

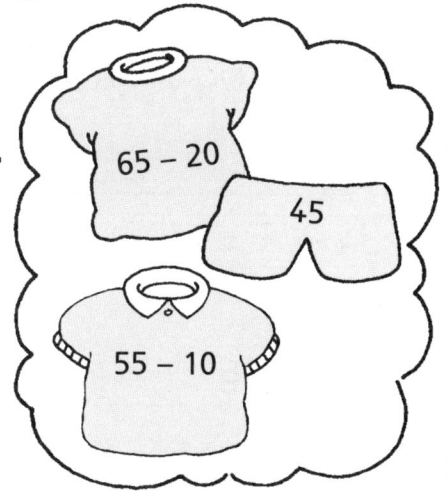

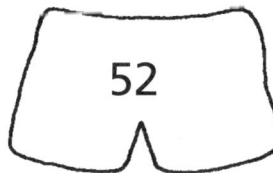

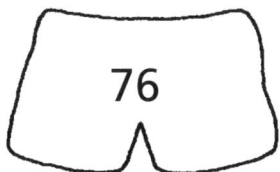

65 – 20

45

55 – 10

33

47

53 – 20

43 – 10

51 – 10

41

57 – 10

86 – 10

96 – 20

72 – 20

52

77 – 20

62 – 10

76

Draw shorts for the missing answer.

Key Skills in Place Value at Key Stage 1
© Paul Broadbent 1998

Subtracting machines

These machines subtract 100.
Write the numbers coming out.

246
357
IN   OUT
290   − 100
465

509
722
IN   OUT
340   − 100
929

187
272
IN   OUT
904   − 100
396

147
211
IN   OUT
109   − 100
704

Write the numbers going in to each machine.

IN   OUT   642
− 100   309
117
48

IN   OUT   23
− 100   140
219
747

Subtracting 100: function machines
including inverses

Name _____

Kites

Round the number in each kite to the nearest ten.
Then join the kite to that number.

Round up numbers ending in 5.

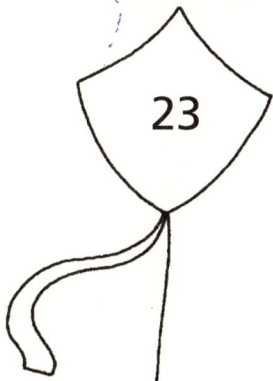

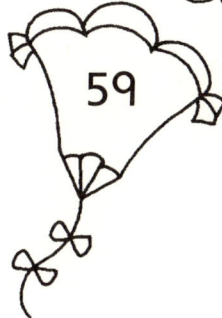

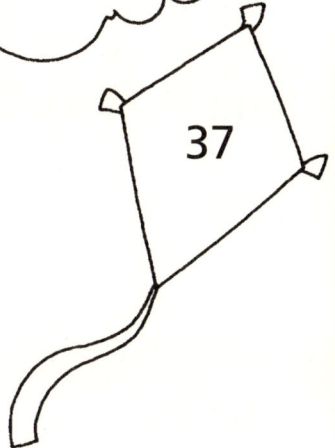

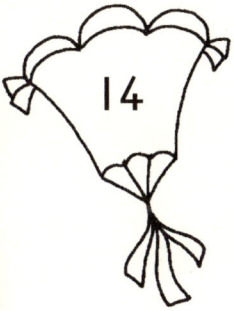

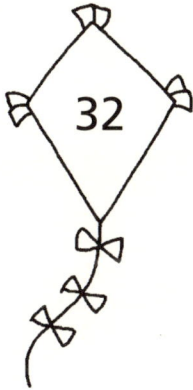

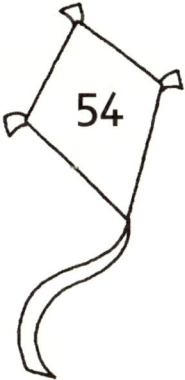

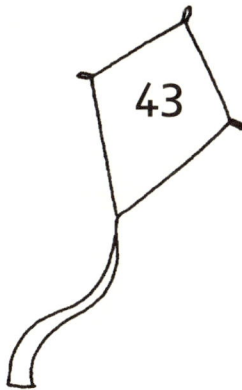

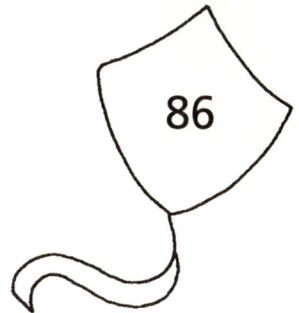

47

23

59

37

14

32

54

75

43

73

65

86

0   10   20   30   40   50   60   70   80   90

Rounding TU numbers to the nearest 10

Key Skills in Place Value at Key Stage 1

Name _____

Fruit and nuts

Round each amount to the nearest ten.

Round up numbers ending in 5.

walnuts 247

raisins 784

hazelnuts 306

cashew nuts 585

642 **sultanas**

983 **currants**

737 **peanuts**

597 **chestnuts**

635 **cob nuts**

Rounding HTU numbers to the nearest 10

Key Skills in Place Value at Key Stage 1
© Paul Broadbent 1998

Fishing

Round each number to the nearest hundred.
Then join the boat to its anchor.

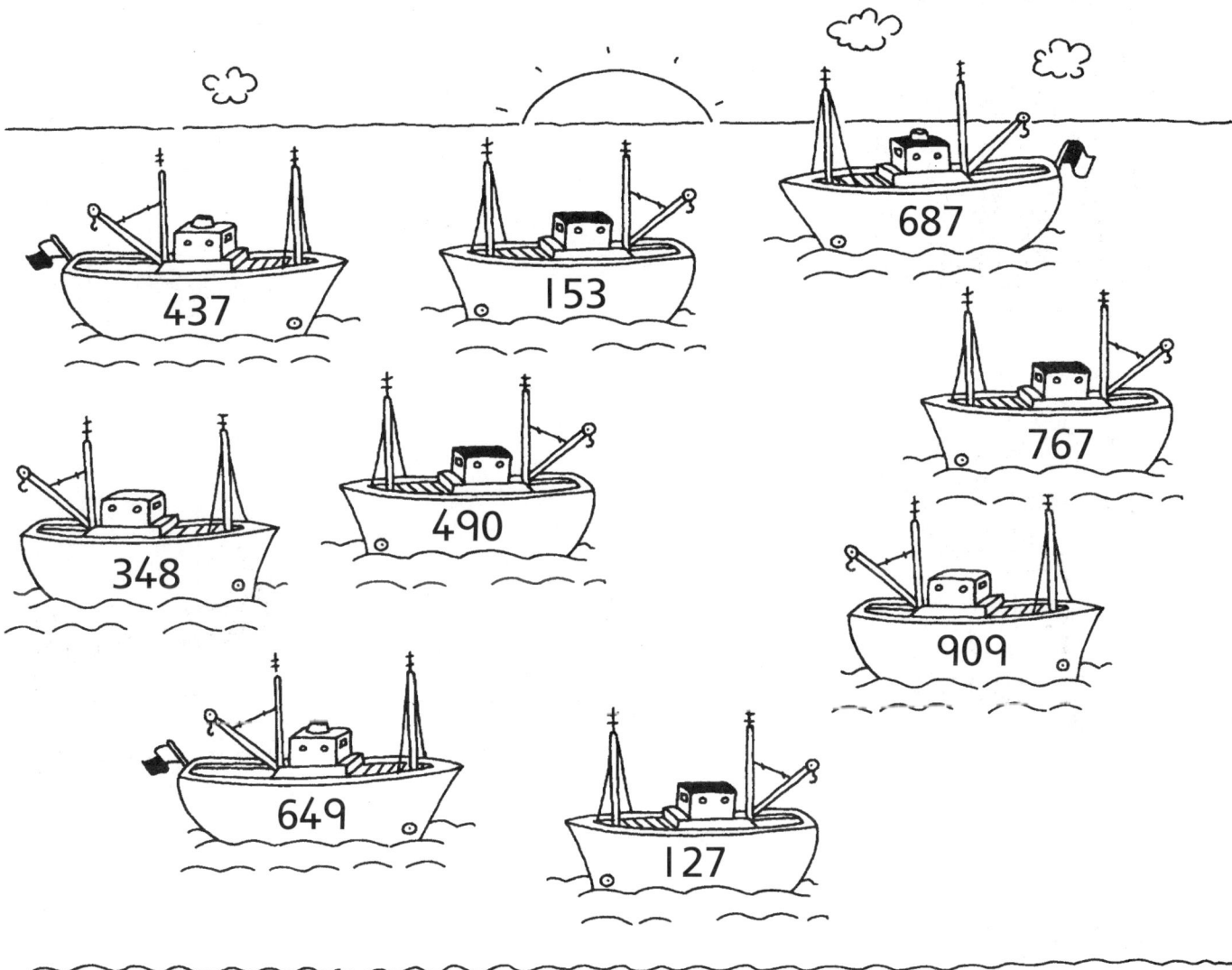

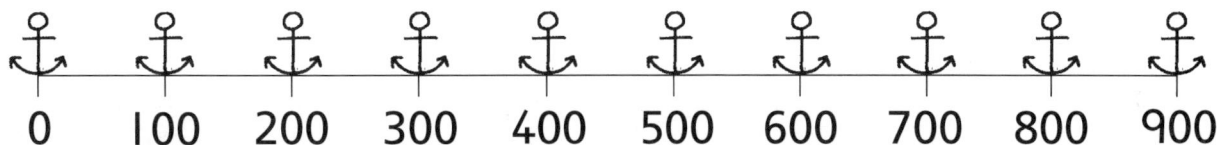

437

153

687

348

490

767

909

649

127

| 0 | 100 | 200 | 300 | 400 | 500 | 600 | 700 | 800 | 900 |

Rounding numbers to the nearest 100

Rounding robots

Round these numbers to the nearest ten and the nearest hundred.

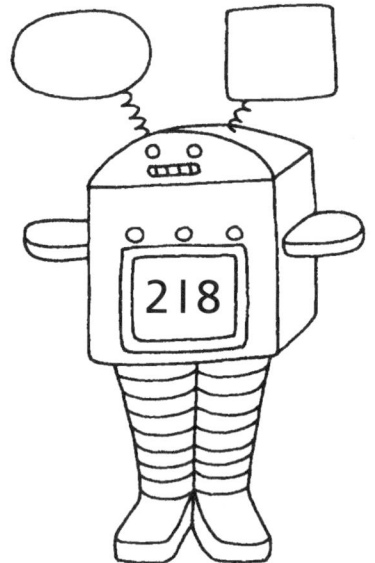

240 nearest 10   200 nearest 100

247

307

652

218

593

185

809

744

Key Skills in Place Value at Key Stage 1
© Paul Broadbent 1998

Name _____

Name _____

Railway stations

Draw a track to join the stations in order.
Start with the smallest number.

13

19

27

36

31

44

40

59

52

68

71

98

78

84

92

Ordering TU numbers

Key Skills in Place Value at Key Stage 1
© Paul Broadbent 1998

Rally cars

Name _____

Write the car numbers in order.
Start with the smallest number.

447

340

470

743

430

703

374

407

smallest   largest

Ordering HTU numbers

Key Skills in Place Value at Key Stage 1
© Paul Broadbent 1998

© Special Copyright Conditions Apply

Name _____

Postcards

Sort the postcards into order.
Start with the smallest number.

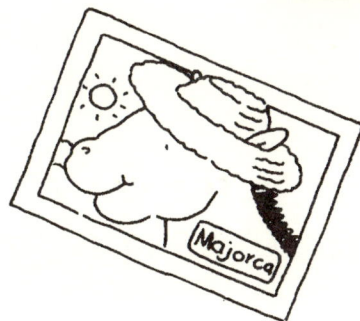

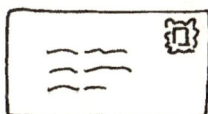

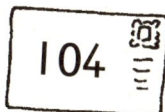

smallest

largest

Ordering numbers

Name _____

Three digits

6   **3**   **8**

Which numbers can be made from these three digits?

Write the numbers in order.
Start with the smallest.

Roll a dice to choose your digits.
Choose three different digits.

Explore the
numbers that
can be made.

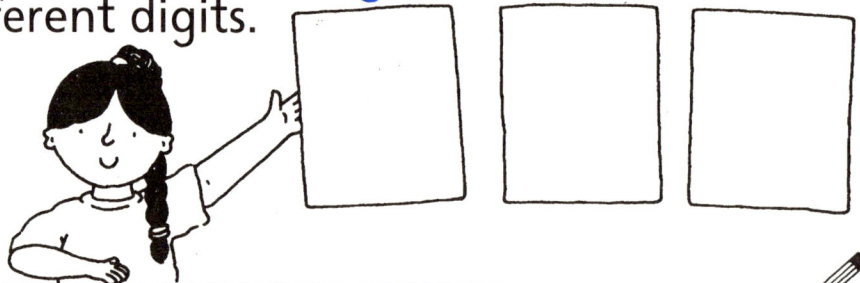

Ordering numbers